Captain Fiddle's Tunes and Variations
Book 1

by Ryan J Thomson

ISBN-13: 978-0-931877-13-1
ISBN-10: 0-931877-13-x

© 2005
Captain Fiddle Publications
Newmarket, New Hampshire

Other offerings from Captain Fiddle Publications

A Folk Musician's Working Guide to Chords, Keys, Scales, more, a book by Ryan Thomson for any instrument and style. - lots of easy "look up" tables: chords, modes and scales, key signatures, circle of fifths, intervals, transposing, musical notation, basic music theory, sharps and flats, rhythms, scale notes for every key, notes for every chord type. See reviews on pg 54.

Waltzes for Folk instruments and Country Dancing - 72 waltzes in standard music notation compiled and arranged by Ryan Thomson for fiddle, mandolin, flute, recorder ,etc., with suggested chords. Includes: Celtic, American, Scandinavian, and European. Written music book includes CD of all 72 tunes.

Fiddle & Violin Buyers Guide - by Ryan Thomson, This illustrated guide saves you money and helps you pick out a good quality fiddle and bow, new or used. It includes: sources for instruments; bow and fiddle selection; examining all parts for quality construction. See reviews on page 54.

Fiddle Contest Kit - Includes complete plans for running a fiddle contest: a contest preparation checklist, publicity ideas, briefing and selection of judges, site setup, sound system, photo copy-ready judging forms, tally sheet and contest rules.

The Fiddlers Almanac - by Ryan Thomson, a hardbound collectors item, includes a CD of fiddle tunes, "This informative and highly readable book is an excellent source book for all would-be fiddle players and a source of further information and reference for players who wish to increase their knowledge and repertoire." - American Library Association.

Banjo Tab Book - 19 tunes in Clawhammer Tablature from the Great Bay Stomp CD, by Ryan Thomson. Book contains transcriptions of the "Great Bay Stomp" CD, illustrations of historical photos, and a description of old-time claw hammer playing techniques. Book and CD available separately or together.
"Highly Listenable," - Old Time Herald.

How to Make and Play Washtub Bass video DVD - by Ryan Thomson, includes: construction details, playing techniques and tips. The washtub bass can be easily built for low cost. It is an amazingly versatile instrument that can be used to play just about any kind of music, in any key. Special wash tub bass string included!   ages 8 to adult

Treatise on the Construction, Preservation, Repair, and Improvement of the Violin - Two separate translations of an 1828 text by Jacob Otto, instrument maker for the Archduke of Weimar. Topics: major violin makers in Europe, theories of violin construction, bringing out violin tone through repair and preservation. Mostly text, a few illustrations.

Moore's Irish Melodies - 27 pieces in standard notation for piano and voice: dance tunes, aires, harmonized vocal arrangements: Moore's biography, Carolan's Concerto, Thady You Gander, Black Joke, Rose Tree, Old Woman, Sly Patrick, more, 8.5 x 11 book.

Captain Fiddle's "Teach Yourself" Fiddle CDs - jigs, reels, hoe downs, hornpipes, and waltzes. Includes accompanying chords. The tunes and variations range from easy to moderately difficult. available with corresponding written music. For beginners or experienced fiddlers wanting to learn new tunes:
"highly recommended..a great collection" - Fiddler Magazine

Chord Encyclopedia - A book of chord charts for 1400 different fiddle tunes organized alphabetically: reels, jigs, hornpipes, waltzes, polkas, hoe downs, old timey, Irish, contra dance, bluegrass, more! For jam sessions, dances, reference. Two sizes - compact 8.5 x 5.5 inch, and large print 8.5 x 11 inch.

From the Ballroom to Hell, A Dancing Masters Experience, by R.F. Henry: A reprint of the original handbook from 1894, illustrated with cartoons depicting "ruined" dancers, and preaches about the "evils" of waltzing and ballroom dancing. A perfect humorous gift.

Fiddling for Beginners - DVD course by Ryan Thomson designed for learners with little or no experience with fiddle or violin playing. No music reading ability is required. Course covers holding the instrument, basic fingering, bowing, rhythms, scales, and tune variations. Included is a 80 minute video DVD, illustrated book with written musical notation.

Swing Fiddle, An Introduction - by Ryan Thomson, bios of many jazz violinists, western swing fiddlers, discography, tips on improvisation, fiddle chords, fingerings, jazz music theory and chords, much more. " Swing Fiddle is written with integrity and objectivity and may be of great interest to those folks wanting an introduction,"....... Strings Magazine

Complete Learn Clawhammer Banjo Kit, includes 2 DVDs, banjo CD, Banjo Tab book.

DVD - Pennywhistle, First Lesson, with Ryan Thomson, for beginners, learn celtic tunes.

DVD - Celtic Wooden Flute, First Lesson, with Ryan Thomson, for beginners, breathing and fingering techniques, teaches a jig, reel, hornpipe, slide, and polka. For simple keyless wooden flute.

DVD - Piano Accompaniment to Fiddlers, First Lesson, for beginners and experienced pianists alike, no music reading required. learn fingerings, inversions, back up patterns.

DVD - Accordion, Jam Session Style, First Lesson, for beginners, how to use the accordion like a guitar to play accompaniment, etc. chording, rhythms, fingerings, much more.

Practical History of the Violin, reprint of 1911 edition, 1200 makers listed, 778 authentic violin labels illustrated, chronological record of makers, biographies.

Modern Quadrille Call Book, reprint of a dance caller's guide from from 1902, includes calls and directions for over 70 dances.

Dobson's New System for Banjo, reprint of 1877 book, 98 banjo tunes in standard notation, instructions and tunings for this finger picking style, tunes range from easy to difficult.

The Clog Dance Book, reprint of an early 20th century clog dancing instruction book, dances range from easy to advanced.

For Left Handers:
Playing Violin and Fiddle Left Handed, a documentary book including facts and references about playing left handed.

Left Handed Fiddling for Beginners, a book and DVD set for left handed fiddling from scratch. no music reading required

DVDs - Left Handed Banjo, Clawhammer Style, complete kit for for beginners, from banjo playing basics through learning tunes.

Visit captainfiddle.com for our latest offerings

Table of Contents

Over the Waterfall

Author's Preface

I originally caught the "Fiddling Bug" while attending contra and square dances and then spent every spare moment soaking in the sea of tunes that I encountered in the Appalachian mountains, at New England country dances, at west coast folk music festivals, during dusk to dawn picking parties, and from the many fiddling friends I've met in the last 30 years.

I've learned some tunes by hearing other fiddlers play them at dances, some from recordings and fiddle contests, and others from written collections of fiddle music. Sometimes I've arranged a tune from several sources: a bit from a recorded version, musical phrases from another local fiddler, and some licks from my own bag of fiddle tricks.

In this series, I've written out tunes which have been some of my favorites over the years. The tunes in this tune book correspond with those on my **"Teach Yourself" fiddle CDs #2 and #3**. On the CDs I play a basic version very slowly, and then several variations at faster tempos.

Many folks turn to a *book* of written music because they want to learn how a tune "goes." One however, has only to listen to two different fiddlers to find out that a tune goes differently depending upon who is playing it! And any individual experienced dance fiddler continually varies a tune while playing it

Still, a book serves the useful purpose of providing a version which is frozen on the printed page. This gives a beginning folk player something solid to hang on to, and the advanced player a platform from which to launch into creative variations.

In New England we play fiddle tunes for country dances which include figures such as squares, contras, quadrilles and waltzes.

Ryan Thomson

© Robert Nilson

During the course of a particular dance the musicians must play continuously for a long period of time. To keep the playing interesting, musicians often play medleys of tunes, sometimes changing keys in the process.

Playing any particular tune over and over without variation may become boring. This depends, however, upon how difficult the tune is to play. Even experienced players can have problems with tunes that they have only recently learned.

It may take every bit of concentration a player has merely to play all of the notes in tune and as quickly as the dance demands. Rather than experiencing boredom, a fiddler may be hard pressed to keep up; beads of sweat break out on the forehead and eyes remain fixed in a static glaze. The fiddler breathes a sigh of relief when the dancers complete their last figures and the caller gives the "going out" signal to stop.

Fiddlers find all tunes easier to play after time. It may become so effortless to play a tune that the fiddler goes on to chewing gum and winking at the whirling dancers on the floor. But don't think that the fiddler is loafing. The hard parts of the tune can still be gauged by watching when the fiddler momentarily stops chewing! (or plays a wrong note in the process of winking!)

The ultimate sign of tune mastery comes when the fiddler can play numerous complex tune variations while simultaneously carrying on an animated conversation with the piano player about the previous night's revels. There's no end to the repertoire though. After each tune is mastered there's always another, with several lifetime's worth of great tunes waiting to be played!

Some fiddlers make dance playing more interesting by learning many variations on

4

preface continued

Some fiddlers make dance playing more interesting by learning many variations on their tunes. These variations can arise from several sources: spontaneously during repetitive playing, from careful pre-arrangement, or from learning a tune by ear and playing it a bit differently than the person it was learned from. In this book and CD collection I've written and played both what I interpret as the "essence" of a tune, and also fun and creative variations on it.

In past times, fiddle tunes were passed along mostly by ear and versions within particular geographic regions tended to be similar. Players who incorporated tasteful variations into their playing were respected. Some people, though, would insist that a particular version, either from a book of fiddle music, or from a certain fiddler was the "correct" or "best," version. The fun in fiddle music comes from the fact that there is no one correct or best way to play any tune. A particular player can shape a tune to fit his or her own fancy.

I would hope that you use this book and set of recordings as a way to get you started down the road, so to speak. I've suggested chords for accompanying instruments. Have fun with these versions. Some of the variations I play, particularly on the "southern" tunes have complex rhythms and phrasing and standard music notation lacks the flexibility to notate them precisely.

I've done the best I can to write them out. This is where listening becomes all important. A proper technique for learning fiddling is to listen to fiddling and to try to duplicate the sound on your own instrument. And then do it again and again! This is the approach used by all master fiddlers when they are learning. In fact, this is fastest and most efficient way to learn improvisation in fiddle tunes. That's because you simultaneously learn variations while you are attempting to play something that you hear another person play.

Your variations will originate primarily from your "mistakes" when you try to imitate the playing of others. You don't get that special bonus when you merely learn from written notes on a page!

About the Author

Ryan Thomson was born in Salt Lake City, Utah, into a family with a fiddling and music heritage stretching back to the pioneer days when his ancesters played fiddles for square dances while traveling west from New England across the praries in covered wagons.

He is a music and dance professional who has been honored by inclusion on the roster of the New Hampshire State Council on the Arts. He is a past winner of the Northeastern Regional award at the National Fiddle Contest and is a multi-instrumentalist who performs and teaches weekly on fiddle, banjo, flute, piano, accordian, pennywhistle and calls dances. In his spare time he plays chamber music in a classical ensemble.

He formerly studied science at San Diego State University, and then topics in the psychology of music in graduate school at the University of New Hampshire. He acquired the nick name "Captain Fiddle," from his co-workers on college radio WUNH where he played his fiddle live on his fiddling and folk music show. He continued on radio with a regular Sunday night show on National Public Radio WEVO.

After college he decided on a music making career and joined a full time Nashville country band, touring the eastern USA, playing fiddle 6 days a week in dance halls and honky tonks. He twice received the nomination for "Country Fiddler of the Year," from the Massachusetts Country Music Association.

In 1985 he founded Captain Fiddle Publications by authoring his first book, The Fiddler's Almanac, a general reference source about fiddlers and fiddling which can be presently found in over 3000 libraries. He has since authored numerous fiddling and fiddle books, recordings, and instructional DVD videos on various musical topics. Ryan's works have received top reviews from the American Library Association and many other music publications.

Ryan was invited as a special guest artist to perform at the Celebrate New Hampshire festival sponsored by the Smithsonian and was invited to tutor fiddle at the Festival of American Fiddle Tunes. He presently lives in New Hampshire and teaches music both at the Phillips Exeter Academy during the school year, and at folk music and dance camps nationally in the summer time.

You can find out about his current activities at captainfiddle.com.

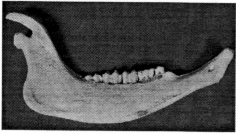

buffalo jaw bone

Angeline The Baker.

I originally learned this traditional tune from mandolin player Kenny Hall. It's a great southern style square dance tune, easy enough for beginners, and fun to play for its liveliness. My version is related to the Stephen Foster song "Angelina Baker" which was published by F.D. Benteen of Baltimore on March 18, 1850. There are similarities in the melody but the version I play is quite different from Foster's, its having been passed along from person to person for many years by ear, and having been adapted to square dance format.

I've also included an arrangement of the original Stephen Foster song introduction (which is very similar to the melody of his verses) combined with his chorus, to fit the style of a typical two-part fiddle tune.

Foster wrote these words in his pseudo negro dialect - " I've seen my Angelina in de spring time and de fall, I've seen her in de cornfield and I've seen her at de ball; and ebry time I met her she was smiling like the sun, but now I'm left to weep a tear cayse Angelina's gone. Angelina Baker! Angelina Baker's gone, She left me here to weep a tear and beat on de old jaw bone."

In those times country musicians sometimes used the actual jaw bone of an ass or other large animal as a percussion and rhythm instrument.

Angeline the Baker, the song

In modern times this tune is common in "old timey" jam sessions.
Typical verses which fit the basic melody in the A part are as follows:

- Angeline the baker, her age is 43. I feed her apples by the peck, but she won't marry me!

- Angeline is handsome, Angeline is tall.
They say she sprained her ankle while dancing at the ball.

- Angelina Baker, Angelina Baker's gone. She left me here to weep a tear and beat on the old jaw bone.

- Father was a baker, they called him Uncle Sam, I never can forget her, no matter where I am.

- Angeline the baker, Angeline I know, Wished I married Angeline twenty years ago.

- Bought Angeline a brand new dress, neither black nor brown, It was the color of a stormy cloud, before the rain pours down.

Angeline the Baker

from slow version on CD

as played by Ryan Thomson

Part A

Part B

Angeline the Baker variations

as played by Ryan Thomson

part A variations

part B variations

Arkansas Traveler

slow version on CD

As played by Ryan Thomson

I bought my first fiddle at a yard sale and this is the very first tune that I tried playing by ear. A fellow fiddler heard me scratching away on the first part of it, and actually recognised the tune within my rendition, giving me great joy! He also pointed out that I was playing a small child's sized instrument, so it wasn't until I got a fiddle of the proper size that I learned the whole thing.

8

Arkansas Traveler. There is a story circulating that in some southern fiddle contests the ability to play this tune was a requirement for entry. Various sources suggest that this classic southern tune may be as old as the 1850's and was first used in a play which featured skits pitting country folk against the up-town city slickers while this tune was being played:

City Slicker: " Farmer, can I take this road to Hillsboro?"
Farmer: " I don't know why you'd want to do that, they've already got a road there."

Arkansas Traveler   as played by Ryan Thomson

Bonaparte's Retreat

Slow version on CD
part A

As played by Ryan Thomson

variations - first version on CD

Bonaparte's Retreat

Bonaparte's Retreat. This was originally a Scottish or Irish bagpipe tune composed by an unknown piper to commemorate Bonaparte's defeat at Waterloo. Old time american fiddlers turned it into a lively square dance tune designed to simulate the sound of bagpipe drones.

Classical composer Aaron Copeland liked the appalachian fiddler's renditions so much that he "borrowed" the melody to use in his composition - Appalachian Spring.

Bonaparte's Retreat variations

Part A (from third version on CD)

As played by Ryan Thomson

Part B

Part B variation(basic melody line)

Part B with double stop accent as on CD

12

Chorus Jig

As played by Ryan Thomson

Chorus Jig. This classic traditional New England tune is not a true jig
as it is in 2/4 time; but uses the word
"jig" as a term referring to dancing.
The tune matches the steps of a popular contra dance of the same name
which starts out with the command:
"Down the outside." It's played ABCB,
ABCB, etc.(the B part comes every
other time), until couples have gone
through all of the figures.
Accompanying musicians play as if
there is only two parts since the A and
C parts have the same chords.

Chorus Jig, the dance

Couples line up, gents in right line, ladies in the left,
across from their partners. Couples are numbered ones and
twos in order from closest to the band. Ones are "active."

(A part music) - Actives down outside, turn alone, and come
back up, meet partner in center.

 - Actives down center, turn alone and back, cast off with
one below.

(B part music) - Turn country corners, balance partner in
center and swing. (actives finish by facing up toward band)

13

Cock of the North

as played by Ryan Thomson

Part A

Part B

substitute either of these measures for the measures marked above.

*1   *2

Cock O' the North. I heard this traditional scottish jig from the popular Irish group, the Chieftains, when I heard them perform it at a concert in Los Angeles. I play it primarily for country dances. The Chieftains played the A and B parts in this same order. I later discovered that some fiddlers reverse the parts, but I like it this way better.

Common lore is that the head(chief) of the Gordon clan became known as "the Cock of the North" in the 16and 17th centuries, because of his power and fame. This tune was supposedly named in honor of him and became the official regimental tune of the Gordon Highlanders. Historians have noted that regimental pipers often played this tune into battles.

Cock of the North

part A variations

as played by Ryan Thomson

part B variations

After I moved to Newmarket, New Hampshire in 1977, I started a series of bi-monthly public contra dances in the old Town Hall. At the first dance there was lots of hooting, hollering and foot stomping, especially foot stomping. Unbeknownst to us, the police station was in a office directly beneath our dance floor.

Evidently our enthusiam was causing a rain of plaster dust from the ceiling to descend upon the heads of the officers below. They weren't happy about that. After the dance they were waiting for us outside in a cruiser. We loaded up our guitar player's car with instruments and equipment and pulled away. The officers came immediately after us with all lights flashing.

After ordering us outside our vehicle they patted us down for concealed weapons, and proceeded to document numerous equipment violations on our guitar players old car. After a time (and payment of fines) we made up and the police officers planned to be out cruising whenever we held our dances.

After several years of lively dancing our old town hall burned down and brought a sad end to our local dances. Fortunately some new dances started up in neighboring towns.

Dickson County Blues

Part A

as played by Ryan Thomson

often missed chord

I learned this tune by ear from a local fiddler who had learned it from a recording of Arthur Smith. I listened carefully, experimented with the bowing and fingering, and finally settled comfortably into my own version. I found it difficult to write out my version precisely in standard musical notation though, so use this music along with some careful listening to the CD. Note that the number of measures in each part exceeds the standard 8 bars of most dance tunes. That means that this tune doesn't work well for square dances.

But its fun to play and to listen to.

Another difficulty is that most accompanying guitarists who are unfamiliar with the tune will have an uncontrolable urge to play the 3rd chord in the B part as an **A**, instead of a **D**.

I've been battling this problem for 30 years. If there isn't time to practice ahead of time I just yell out, "D chord coming up... HERE!, stay on the D, A chord coming up... NOW!)

Dickson County is in the state of Tennessee.

16

Drowsy Maggie

As played by Ryan Thomson

Drowsy Maggie. This traditional tune is a staple of the Irish fiddler's diet since it is one of the most requested tunes by those with a wee bit of familiarity with traditional fiddle tunes. It sounds good played fast. In irish style each part is played only once, which is too short for many country dances. The solution for dance playing is to double up each part.

Its a special tune because it is full of driving energy when played by an experienced musician, yet is fun to play even by a beginner. Learn it more quickly and efficiently by practicing twice as long on the harder second part than the easier first part!

17

Eskimo Waltz

also Upic, Ootpic, Oopik, etc.

As played by Ryan Thomson

part A

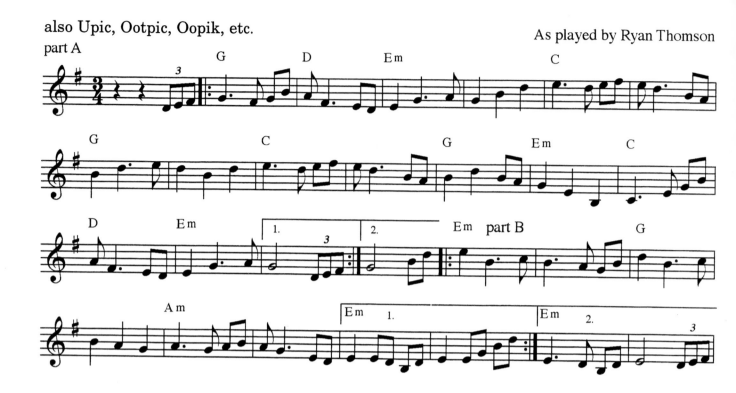

part A variations

Eskimo Waltz. I learned this tune in Idaho during a week long jam session at the National Fiddle Contest in 1978. I had driven straight there one summer after my last class day of the year at the University of New Hampshire. The contest was held in the Weiser High School gym and I pitched my tent in the middle of the football field to be near the center of the action. The music went on around me almost 24 hours a day and by the end of the week my fiddle had learned a number of new tunes, including this beautiful waltz that I heard a lady fiddler play in the contest.

Gentle Maiden Waltz

part A (twice with variations)

As played by Ryan Thomson

part B (twice with variations)

Gentle Maiden Waltz. This is another beautiful traditional waltz of Irish origin suitable for New England style country dancing. It's the first waltz I learned on the fiddle and reminds me of the outdoor summer contra dances that I organized at San Diego State University in the early 1970's. I learned many fiddle tunes by first dancing to them and then finding the notes on my fiddle after I was familiar with the melodies by hearing other fiddlers play them.

La Bastringue

part A (slow version on CD)

As played by Ryan Thomson

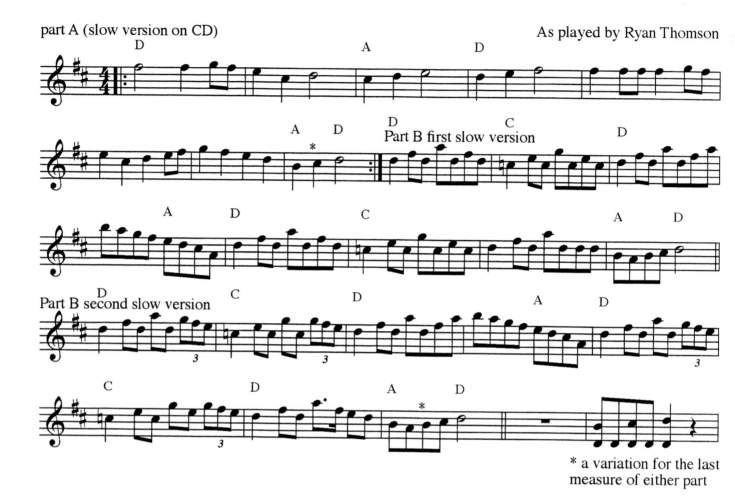

Part B first slow version

Part B second slow version

* a variation for the last measure of either part

La Bastringue means "the triangle," and according to a french canadian source, the word itself is·an imitation of the sound that the triangle makes. The triangle is played in French influenced cajun music from Louisiana, but not much in French music from Canada from which this version came, even though both musics were influenced by the French acadian population of the 1700's in Nova Scotia.

I learned this traditional french canadian tune by ear from a record of the playing of Jean Carignan. I've included a basic version of the tune, and also some of the fancier licks and double stops I put into the tune when I really get going. I tend to use " up" bows often on the beat, contrary to the general practice of most violin players to play down bows on the beat. As a self taught fiddler I never thought about this much until I jammed with southern style fiddler Tommy Jarrell in his kitchen in North Carolina. He asked me to play a tune. I played him this tune, and he then remarked, "you're an up bow fiddler!"

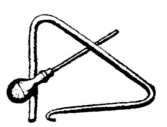

La Bastringue

Variations on the tune (from first and third versions on CD)

My old contra and square dance band, The Last Chance String Band, used to do lots of barn dances. Once in the dead of a February New Hampshire winter we were asked to play for a dance in the next town over from Newmarket. So we drove over to Durham and located the barn in the agricultural section of the University at Durham.

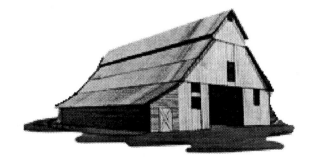

It was a bit cool that evening, about 5 degrees above zero. The old wooden barn had a dirt floor, but someone had fashioned a stage from old timbers and planks. We situated ourselves on stage, dressed in several layers of flannel, wool, and topped off with down parkas. After the caller had taught each dance and it became time to play, we removed our gloves and thrashed through lively jigs and reels.

There was quite a large crowd of enthusiastic college kids, and after an hour or so of vigorous dancing the combined body heat brought the inside temperature up to the mid 40's, and we removed our parkas to play, feeling quite toasty!

Mary's (Mairi's) Wedding

part A slow version on CD

As played by Ryan Thomson

part B slow version on CD

part A variations

part B variations

part A variations

Mary's Wedding. (The original gaelic spelling is "Mairi") This traditional untitled melody is found in the Marjorie Kennedy-Fraser collection of music of the Hebrides, published in the early 20th century. It is sometimes also known as the Lewis Bridal March. The Hebrides Islands are off the west coast of Scotland.

Johnny Bannerman wrote the original lyrics to this melody in Gaelic for Mary McNiven in 1935. (although not actually for her wedding) The words were translated into english soon after and the song became wildly popular in scottish circles.

I've written the melody out in two versions: the basic melody, and then with double stops to simulate bagpipe drones. For a dance we double the parts as written, but singers don't repeat the parts.

Mairi's Wedding, the song (in English)

Chorus:
    Step we gaily, on we go, heel for heel, toe for toe arm in arm and on we go, all for Mairi's Wedding.

Verses:
- Over hillways up and down, myrtle green and bracken brown, past the sheiling through the town, all for sake of Mairi.
- Plenty herring plenty meal, plenty peat to fill her creel, plenty bonny bairns as weel, that's the toast for Mairi.
- Cheeks as bright as rowans are, brighter far than any star, fairest of them all by far, is my darling Mairi.

Margaret's Waltz

by Pat Shaw

as played by Ryan Thomson

part A

Englishman Pat Shaw composed Margaret's Waltz as both a tune and a dance, for Margaret Grant on her retirement in 1959 as English Folk and Country Dance Society representative in Devon. I learned it by ear partly from the hammered dulcimer playing of Bill Spence, and partly by fiddler Aly Bain on a record from the 1970's. I play it often at contra dances, not the formal dance by Pat Shaw, but for folks who just want to waltz continuously.

Margaret's Waltz, the dance (by Pat Shaw)

Dancers face each other and "advance & retire" (forward and back)

Each person of a couple turns the other with a right hand back to where each started from,

Repeat turns with left hands
ladies chain across (two adjacent couples face each other and ladies only take right hands, and walk past each other to each other's place)

couples chassez both to right & left (sort of a gallop by a couple)

star to place (two couples face and all individuals place right hands in center, turning in a "star" formation back to place.

do-si-do opposite (pass by right shoulders the person you face, move sideways around behind them, and then back up to place.)

each couple waltzes till the end of the tune

repeat all figures till the band stops!

Margaret's Waltz variations

by Pat Shaw

as played by Ryan Thomson

Some scholars point out the similarities of the waltz to earlier social dances such as the "landler." According to historian John Funk the origin of the waltz can be traced back to Germany, Austria, Bavaria, and Bohemia. He notes that the earliest known use of the german word "walzen" being associated with music in triple time (3/4) was in 1754. In 1774 Goethe used the term "waltzing" to describe a dance in which a couple "circled around each other like spheres."

In 1797 Beethoven published his Twelve German Dances," and was the first major composer to designate the term "waltz" for a solo piano piece in 3/4. All social classes danced in this era though, and so country musicians also composed tunes for waltzing. In any case, the waltz became very popular, spreading to America and England. It was danced at different tempos, depending upon locality.

In Vienna people danced a fast version while in america it was slower. Composers wrote waltzes which conformed to these varying dance speeds. As a folk dance musician I often vary my waltz playing speed depending upon the wishes of the dancers I am playing for.

My Love is but a Lassie

as played by Ryan Thomson

Variations

as played by Ryan Thomson

My love is but a Lassie. This traditional Scottish tune is also known as "O'er too young to marry." It has a bouncy feel and is good for dances with much galloping and cavorting about. The oldest reference to it that I could find was in a tune collection compiled in 1800 to 1802 by William

Litten, a sailor in the British India fleet. Many sailing vessels had "ship's fiddlers," to entertain the crew and help make the work lighter. I've often wondered how the fiddlers managed to keep their fiddles in one piece under constant conditions of dampness aboard ship which would cause the glue joints to soften and separate.

Off She Goes

part A (slow version on CD)

As played by Ryan Thomson

part B (slow version on CD)

part A variations

part B variations

Off She Goes: A popular traditional Scottish jig, common in scottish, irish, and american contra dance repertoires.

26

Old French

Old French. This fine traditional French Canadian reel is well suited for dancing. The accompaniment for it is in the key of D in the A part and the key of A in the B part. I learned it after listening to it many times at New England country dances. It sounds good at a fast pace and has the lively rhythms common to French dance tunes.

Old Joe Clark

As played by Ryan Thomson

slow version on CD

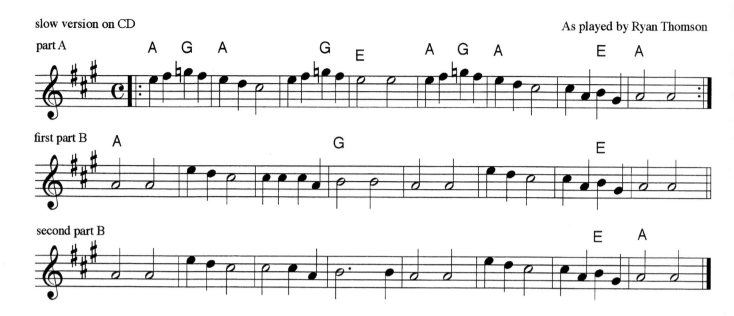

part A

first part B

second part B

Old Joe Clark This traditional southern tune is a must for the southern style fiddler's square dance or clogging repertoire. Its a good example of the type of tune that has enough inherent rhythm within it that old time fiddlers can play it un-accompanied for square dancers or cloggers. It sounds good at any speed from medium to lightning fast.

a clogger

Old Joe Clark, the song

Some verses (which fit the melody of the A part):

- I wish I had a nickel, I wish I had a dime, I wish I had a pretty girl to kiss and call her mine.

- I went down to Old Joe's house, he invited me to supper, I stumped my toe on the table leg and stuck my nose in the butter.

- Old Joe Clark had a house, fifteen stories high, and every story in that house was filled with chicken pie.

- I used to live on mountain top, But now I live in town, I'm boarding at the big hotel, courting Betsy Brown.

- Old Joe Clark he built a house, took him 'bout a week, he built the floor above his head, and the ceiling under his feet

The chorus fits the B part of the tune:

"Round, round, Old Joe Clark, round, round I say, round, round, Old Joe Clark, I'm a going away."

Old Joe Clark - part A variations

part A variations

As played by Ryan Thomson

part A variations

part A variations

part A variations

part A variations

Old Joe Clark - part A variations continued

part A variations

As played by Ryan Thomson

*

Old Joe Clark part B variations

part B variations

part B variations

part B variations (goes with part A above *)

30

Old Molly Hare

slow version on CD

as played by Ryan Thomson

Variations

as played by Ryan Thomson

Old Molly Hare. This is a traditional southern Appalachian square dance tune derived from an older scottish reel. It's a good example of a tune in which the fiddle supplies both a melody and the rhythm for dancing. In dance fiddling there is always a trade off between melody and rhythm. When the bowed rhythm is fancy the melody must be simpler and vice versa.

Old Molly Hare, the song
Verses which fit over the A part of the tune:

 - Old Molly Hare, whatcha doing there?, sitting by the fireside munching on a bear.

 - Old Molly Hare, whatcha doing there? running through the woods just as fast as I can tear.

- Old Molly Hare, whatcha doing there? sitting by the butter dish picking out a hair.

Chorus, B part: Step back, step back, daddy shot a bear, shot him through the eyes and never touched a hair.

One Hundred Pipers

I learned this traditional tune by ear from various sources, mostly from hearing other dance fiddlers. Besides the basic melody I've included versions with double stops to simulate the droning sound of the bagpipes. I've always thought that the tune sounded a lot like bagpipes when played this way, but I was reassured when someone rushed up to me after a performance and asked: "How did you make your fiddle sound exactly like bagpipes?" Bagpipes were around for hundreds of years before fiddles were invented and many fiddle tunes are derived from much older bagpipe tunes. Scottish pipes have a limited range of notes that they can play and so the corresponding fiddle tune versions have the same limitations.

Personal experience has demonstrated the power of the pipes to me. While in college I decided to take a bicycle trip from San Diego to San Francisco with a friend. We carried sleeping bags and camped out in woodsy areas along the way. One Sunday morning we awoke at dawn in the Los Angeles suburbs to continue our ride north. The streets were almost deserted at this time, but after a while I heard the faint sound of piping in the distance. We rode our bikes toward the sound, and rode, and rode, taking various turns and roads as the sound grew louder. We covered several miles before discovering a lone piper marching in the huge empty parking lot of a shopping mall. His motive was clear to us. Where else could you practice bagpipes on an early Sunday morning?

Bagpipes have special drone pipes that play only one continuous tone while the melody changes as it is being fingered on the chanter. This effect is easily imitated on the fiddle because the bow can play two strings at the same time, and one can be fingered while the other unfingered string plays a continuous tone.

In the southern appalachian mountains of the US where scottish imigrants settled, they played many fiddle tunes with such drone effects. In addition, the five string banjo which often accompanied the fiddle also has a drone string, so that the two instruments are perfectly suited to play together. For some reason or other though, jigs were rarely played, and reels in the time of 4/4 were the rhythm of choice in the mountains.

About Bagpipes

Historian Gordon Kinnie has found that the earliest reference to the bagpipe is from Aristophanes, a poet from Athens, Greece, in 425 BC. He describes the enemies of Athens as blowing on a pipe with a bag of dog skin and a chanter made from bone. The 6th century historian, Procpius, mentions the bagpipe as an instrument of the Roman infantry.

Two major competing theories explain the introduction of bagpipes into Scotland: from irish colonization, or from invading Roman legions. A third possibility is that the pipes were invented independently. Their use in Scotland by the end of the 12th century has been documented. Records show that in the early 1500's a number of scottish cities had public pipers who were paid for their services.

Piping was developed into a high art form in Scotland and achieved the level of 'classical" music a hundred years before the piano was invented. The gaelic term for this music was Piobaireachd, pronounced P'broch. The bagpipes are unequalled in their use in military battle, their penetrating sound being able to carry for several miles.

During the rebellion of 1745 The english town of Carlisle surrendered to Scottish Prince Charles Edward Stuart (Bonnie Prince Charlie). Lore has it that he entered either that city, or Edinburgh with his army preceded by one hundred pipers, 32 of his own, and the rest from other clans.

Musicologists have found that bagpipes have been played in many other regions as well, including Russia, Finland, Germany, France, Spain, and Bulgaria. As violins became highly developed in the late 1600's and early 1700's, much of the music played on pipes was transfered over to this portable and versatile instrument.

One Hundred Pipers

part A(slow version on CD)

As played by Ryan Thomson

Over the Waterfall

slow version on CD

as played by Ryan Thomson

Variations

Over the Waterfall. This traditional tune was "discovered" by a tune collector in the southern Appalachian mountains. I learned it first on the banjo, and then transferred it to the fiddle. Its a popular old timey tune because it's easy to play, yet can be made as fancy as desired with rhythmical bowings and double stops. It is distinguished by the "C" chord which occurs in the A part, which is unusual for tunes in the key of D. In pop music this feature is described as a "musical hook," which catches the attention of the listener. I've overheard the following verse:

"I'm going over the waterfall, there's nothing I can do, I'm going over the waterfall, I'm taking my shampoo."

Over the Waterfall variations

as played by Ryan Thomson

part A variation

part B variation

part B variation

part A variation

Rag Time Annie

part A slow version without double stops as played on CD

As played by Ryan Thomson

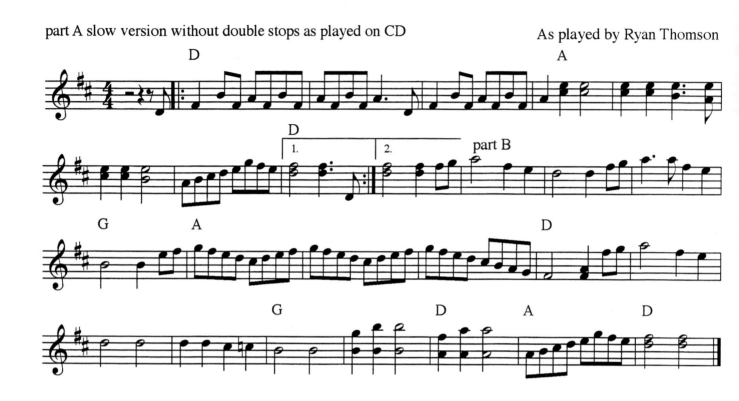

part A with double stops and variations

Ragtime Annie. This traditional southern hoedown is often played at fiddle contests as a show piece but it also makes good square or contra dance music. There are lots of variations floating about, including 3rd and 4th parts in different keys but I've included a basic version as many dance fiddlers play it since two parts is just perfect for a contra dance. Being self taught on fiddle, I made up my version by attempting to recreate the essence of how I heard other players playing it. My own style is use the bow in an upward direction on the beat, which is opposite of how most trained violinists would play. I find that when I do this I have better control of entering in and out of double stops using drone strings while playing at fast tempos.

part A variations for 1st 8 measure section

part A variations for 1st 8 measure section

part B variations

Rights of Man

part A (slow version on CD)

As played by Ryan Thomson

Rights of Man. A traditional tune with a political message, this celtic horn-pipe sounds best played at a slower tempo. Some say that it was written to commemorate Thomas Paine's rebuttal to Burke regarding the French Revolution. Paine's book, *The Rights of Man,* published in 1791, is considered by many to be the first complete statement of republican ideals. His ideas fueled the fires of democracy in young America.

Road to Boston

As played by Ryan Thomson

part A

part B

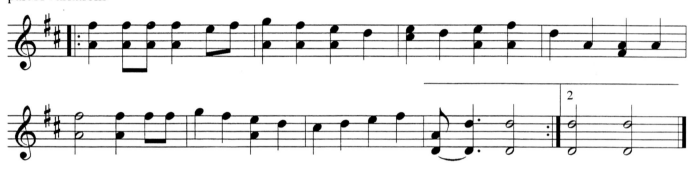

part A variations

part B variations

Road to Boston. This was a popular marching tune of the revolutionary war played on fife and drum, and is still a common tune at country dances in New England. Its easy to play on most any folk instrument.

I can drive to Boston in about an hour and a half from my house in New Hampshire on US Rt 1 which is also still called "Boston Road," but it would have probably taken 2-3 days by foot in 1776.

39

Road to Lisdoonvarna

As played by Ryan Thomson

As played by Ryan Thomson

This traditional tune, and others in the time of 12/8 are described as "single jigs," a distinction which is important to irish dancers whose dance steps correspond to the phrasing of the tunes. The difference between a single jig and a more common "double jig" in 6/8 time is that the phrases of the melody in 12/8 are in chunks twice the size as the chunks in a 6/8 tune. Its still possible to use a 12/8 tune for contra dancing by putting it in a medley with other jigs in 6/8 time. In fact, going from a single jig to a double in the course of the dance gives a visible lift to the motion of the dancers.

Lisdoonvarna is a town in County Clare, Ireland, and is named after the enclosure of a nearby ancient earthern fort, ("Lios Duin Bhearna" in gaelic). The town is fairly new by Irish standards, dating from the start of the nineteenth century. Its well known for its natural sulpher springs and the health spa built around the springs which make it a tourist attraction. The town is also known for match making and a place to which bachelor farmers would travel in search for wives.

This sprightly Irish jig should be in every fiddler's tune list!

Rory O'More

As played by Ryan Thomson

Rory O'More was my first complete fiddle tune! I learned it by dancing the contra dance of the same name while the fiddlers played it. I listened to it carefully in order to remember it, and then found the notes on my own fiddle when I got home. The dance and tune was published in the Atholl Collection of Scottish Dance Music in 1884.

A song using the melody was composed by Samuel Lover in 1961 that starts out like this: "Young Rory O'More courted Kathaleen Bawn, he was bold as a hawk, and she soft as the dawn, he wish'd in his heart pretty Kathleen to please and he tho't the best way to do that was to tease..."

Rory O' More, the dance

dance set up - Couples in long line, men on the right, ladies on the left. Gents 1,4,7 (actives) cross over and change places with their partners.

dance figures -
(Part A music) active couples cross over, down outside below two couples.
then come up the center, cross to place and cast off with original couple below.
Actives give right hand to partner and balance.
Step two steps to right(past each other), join left hands and balance again.
(Part B music) Swing country corners, actives balance and swing partner to place.

Rory O'More, the history

Rory O More was a conspirator against the british in the Irish rebellion of 1641. The situation was very complicated and based upon conflicts of interest between the scots, irish, and british in regards to economic and religious issues. Scotland had revolted against King Charles in 1640 but sided with members of the british parliment against both the irish, and the King, whom they believed shared religious views with the irish.

The irish harvest had been poor, and the british had raised the taxes in Ireland. Members of the british parliment and the scots had been publically advocating the invasion of Ireland and confiscation of irish owned land in order to suppress the population and regious activities.

In response, the conspirators, mostly a group of irish land owners, meant to seize the castle at Dublin in the name of King Charles and then issue their demands for better conditions from the british government, including legal rights denied them because of their religion. Unfortunately their plot was discovered ahead of its planned execution.

The situation quickly got out of the control of the original conspirators. The british sent in a military force to subdue the irish population while the irish retaliated by attacking british and scottish settlers. Much loss of life resulted as the two sides battled.

Rose Tree

as played by Ryan Thomson

The Rose Tree. This traditional polka from County Kerry in Ireland is a common New England contra dance tune. An old English song known as "A False Knight upon the Road" borrows the melody, and the tune is also used in english Morris dancing. My version, which I learned by ear, matches closely the written version I have in my 1852 edition of Moore's Irish Melodies.

42

Sheebeg Sheemore

Entire version on CD

As played by Ryan Thomson

Shebheg and Sheemore. (Si´Bheag Si´Mho´r) This Irish air was composed in the late 1600's by the celebrated harpist Turlough O'Carolan (1670 - 1738). It is said to commemorate a mythological battle between two hosts of "little people" at Sheebeg Shimore(Big Hill Little Hill), which are two "fairy hills" in County Leitrim, Ireland. Sheebeg is supposed to contain the remains of the legendary irish hero Fion Mac Cumhaill. I play the tune in waltz time for dances, and a slower version as a processional piece for weddings.

Carolan became blind at the age of 18 through contracting small pox. He studied harp for three years at the end of which time he was given a harp, a horse, and some money to begin his career as a harper. For the next 45 years he traveled throughout Ireland composing tunes for his patrons. He married Mary Maguire and had seven children.

Smash the Windows

As played by Ryan Thomson

Smash the Windows. This traditional tune is a lively Irish jig which I play for New England country dancing. "Smash the Windows" is an old slang term for "roaring jelly." (nitro glycerine, or dynamite)

44

Soldier's Joy

slow version on CD

traditional, as played by Ryan Thomson

part A

part B first slow variation

part B second slow variation

Soldier's Joy. This traditional tune has Irish origins and is named the "King's Head" in some old Irish tunebooks. It's most commonly played in this country as a southern square dance tune. There is a song to the melody reputed to be from the civil war era with verses as follows:

- I'm gonna get a drink, don't you want to go?, I'm gonna get a drink, don't you want to go?, I'm gonna get a drink, don't you want to go?, home on soldier's joy!

- Its 15 cents for the morphine, 25 cents for the beer, 15 cents for the morphine, going to take me away from here!

- There's a grasshopper sittin' on a sweet potato vine, a grasshopper sittin' on a sweet potato vine, grasshopper sittin' on a sweet potato vine, 'long comes a chicken and says you're mine!

Soldier's Joy

third version on the CD

first part A

As played by Ryan Thomson

second part A

first part B

second part B

first part A

second part A

continues next page

46

Soldiers Joy

Tennessee Waltz

first version on CD

as played by Ryan Thomson

About the tune

Early on in my fiddling career this tune was banned from most fiddle contests because it was considered too new, and not a "traditional" tune. Now that it is long out of general public fashion, most fiddlers are hearing it for the first time as an instrumental piece, liking it, and learning it to play for dances or in contests.

The tune itself was composed in 1950 by Frank "Pee Wee" King, who led a popular western swing band. Redd Stewart wrote words to it and it became a pop song hit on national commercial radio. I learned it just by hearing it many times, mostly by singer Patti Page, and also by Elvis Presley. With the lyrics attached it became the fourth official state song of Tennessee in 1965. (yes, there are three other "tennessee" state songs as well)

It is rarely sung at dances I play for, as the melody itself serves just fine for dancing and the tune plays well on the fiddle. Singers often like it in the key of C, but for dances we like G because we can use the lowest register of the violin

Tennessee Waltz, the song

I was dancin' with my darlin' to the Tennessee Waltz
When an old friend I happened to see.
I introduced her to my loved one
And while they were dancin'
My friend stole my sweetheart from me.

I remember the night and the Tennessee waltz.
Now I know just how much I have lost.
Yes I lost my little darlin' the night
they were playing the beautiful Tennessee waltz.

Tennessee Waltz

second version on CD

as played by Ryan Thomson

part A

part B

Turkey in the Straw

part A (slow version on CD)

As played by Ryan Thomson

part B (slow version on CD)

part A variations

part B variations

Turkey in The Straw. An old refrain for the B part of this traditional tune goes: "Turkey in the Straw, ha ha ha, Turkey in the hay, hey hey hey, bullfrog danced with my mother in law, play a little tune called Turkey in the Straw. The version I've written here is in the key of D. I like this key since there is a high note way up the neck of the fiddle on the B part where the turkey is in the hay. This is a common southern square dance tune and every fiddle player will receive numerous requests for it. I recommend that every concert violinist learn this tune.

West Fork Gals

as played by Ryan Thomson

West Fork Gals. I learned this traditional tune during all-night jams in the southern mountains of West Virginia where it originated. It is often used as a clogging or square dance tune. It sounds great as a fiddle and clawhammer banjo duet.

One day I sat down and figured out that I have spent over a full year of my life in West Virginia on trips to learn fiddle tunes and make music. I've spent most of my time at the Augusta Heritage Center or the Cliff Top festival. All serious folk musicians know that the maximum amount of learning comes from playing music with other people as much and as often as possible.

51

West Fork Gals

part A variations

as played by Ryan Thomson

part B variations

part B variations

part A variations

Whiskey Before Breakfast

Whiskey Before Breakfast. This is another traditional southern style tune that I learned by ear from Kenny Hall while I was living in California. Although I like the tune, I don't advocate the message. Breakfast should certainly come first.

Reviews

The Fiddle and Violin Buyer's Guide, by Ryan Thomson:

"It does provide a handy introduction to the world of instrument dealers and the process of selecting an instrument." - American String Teachers Association

"What will help you on your fiddle-hunting expeditions is to take along a knowledgeable friend and a copy of the Fiddle and Violin Buyer's Guide. Ryan Thomson, the author of several other fiddle-related books, wants to help people find the best fiddles that they can afford, and to that end, he's packed a wealth of information, advice, and insight into this handy little book." - Bluegrass Unlimited

Folk Musician's Working Guide to Chords, Keys, Scales and more, by Ryan Thomson:

"Fiddler's Crossings's resident theory dunce found this book quite helpful in clearing away the fogs of mystery surrounding these topics. The fact that it was written by a fiddler made it easier to understand, and it is written as if you were starting from the very beginning. A very helpful book." - Fiddler's Crossing

"This little gem of a book is perfect for those who may be just learning to play an instrument and wish to find an easily accessible way of understanding the theory and structure behind the music. The book essentially makes it easier for anyone interested in playing folk music either alone or in a group to understand what they are playing and why. Ryan Thomson presents discussions on chord structure, scales, keys, transposing, time signatures, and much more.

It's a good start for someone new to music and a good refresher for others who were discouraged with a heavy handed approach to music theory. Thomson writes is a casual logical style and adds plenty of easy to decipher diagrams." - Dirty Linen Folk, Traditional, and World Music:

"As the wife of a musician, I have spent countless hours listening to various musicians and would-be musicians jam in my living room or garage. Ryan Thomson's book is a great resource for aspiring performers who are serious enough to look past the jam session.

With user friendly text, simply drawn graphics and an unabashed enthusiasm for music, Thomson addresses (among many other things) the complexities of chords, how folk instruments are related by keys, and the uses of the capo - and in less than 100 pages. As the author of nine other books on music and an acomplished player himself, Thomson is more than qualified to lead." - Ex Libris NH Writers and Publishers Project

CD 2

1. Road to Boston
   2. Learn Road to Boston
   3. Learn 100 Pipers
4. 100 Pipers
   5. Learn Mairi's Wedding
6. Mairii's Wedding
   7. Learn Soldier's Joy
8. Soldier's Joy
9. Tennessee Waltz
   10. Learn Old Molly Hare
11. Old Molly Hare
   12. Learn The Rose Tree
13. Rose Tree
   14. Learn Cock of the North
15. Cock of the North
16. Tuning your strings
   17. Learn My Love is but a Lassie
18. My Love is but a Lassie
   19. Learn Road to Lisdoonvarna
20. Road to Lisdoonvarna
21. Margaret's Waltz
   22. Learn Dixon County Blues
23. Dixon County Blues
   24. Learn Off She Goes
25. Off She Goes
   26. Learn Angeline the Baker
27. Angeline the Baker
   28. Learn over the Waterfall
29. Over the Waterfall
30. Gentle Maiden Waltz

CD 3

1. Introduction, tune your strings
   2. learn Old Joe Clark
3. Old Joe Clark
   4. Learn Arkansas Traveler
5. Arkansas Traveler
   6. Learn Whiskey Before Breakfast
7. Whiskey Before Breakfast
   8. Learn West Fork Gals
9. West Fork Gals
10. Oopick(Eskimo) Waltz
   11. Learn Bonaparte's Retreat
12. Bonaparte's Retreat
   13. Learn Rag Time Annie
14. Rag Time Annie
   15. Learn Turkey in the Straw
16. Turkey in the Straw
   17. Learn La Bastringue
18. La Bastringue (The Triangle)
   19. Learn Old French
20. Old French
   21. Learn Rory O'More
22. Rory O'More
   23. Learn Chorus Jig
24. Chorus Jig
   25. Learn Smash the Windows
26. Smash the Windows
   27. Learn Drowsy Maggie
28. Drowsy Maggie
29. Shee Beg Shee Mor
   30. Learn Rights of Man
31. Rights of Man